A DAY THAT MADE HISTORY

THE BATTLE OF HASTINGS

Amanda Clarke

Dryad Press Limited   London

Contents

THE EVENTS

THE INVESTIGATION

Acknowledgments

The author and publishers thank the following for their kind permission to reproduce copyright illustrations: The Armouries, H.M. Tower of London, page 45; Rosemary Booth, page 30; The British Library, pages 33, 46; Peter Clarke, pages 10, 11, 15, 17, 19, 31, 32, 57, 58; English Heritage, pages 7, 56; Living Images, page 59 (left); The Museum of London, pages 47, 49; National Portrait Gallery, page 59 (right); The Victoria and Albert Museum (courtesy of Phaidon Press), pages 1, 3, 4, 5, 18, 21, 25, 27, 35, 37, 48, 54.

Cover photograph: The English shieldwall under attack, from the Bayeux Tapestry (photo: Michael Holford).

Title page picture: William lifts his visor to show his retreating men he is still alive (photo: Victoria and Albert Museum, courtesy of Phaidon Press).

The "Day that Made History" series was devised by Nathaniel Harris.

© Amanda Clarke 1988. First published 1988.
Typeset by Tek-Art Ltd, Kent, and printed and bound by Richard Clay Ltd, Chichester, Sussex for the publishers, Dryad Press Limited, 8 Cavendish Square, London W1M 0AJ

ISBN 0 8521 9755 1

THE
EVENTS

The Normans arrive

The invasion fleet

For an entire month the sea conditions in the Channel had been atrocious, as northerly winds swept down from Scandinavia, causing unseasonal storms and bad weather. But on 27th September, 1066, the winds suddenly changed direction and a southerly blew up from the Continent. This important change was the signal for great activity in the harbour of St-Valéry-sur-Somme, where William, Duke of Normandy, and a large invasion fleet were waiting patiently for the right conditions in which to set sail for England. With the winds favourable at last, embarkation immediately got under way.

The Bayeux Tapestry, worked between 1067 and 1082, gives a vivid visual description of how the ships were loaded with men, weapons, provisions and horses. In his account of events, written in 1073, William of Poitiers, the Duke's chaplain, tells of the general excitement as "all rushed on

Five scenes from the Bayeux Tapestry.

The first shows the coronation of Harold, who was crowned King of England on 6th January, 1066, by Stigand, Archbishop of Canterbury. On the left, Harold is being offered the crown. In the centre, he is holding the orb and sceptre, traditional symbols of monarchy. On the right, the people acclaim the new King.

This scene shows the appearance of a comet, which was taken as an ominous portent for King Harold. The Anglo-Saxon Chronicle records that in April 1066 "a portent such as men had never seen before was seen in the heavens. Some declared the star was a comet, which some called the 'long-haired star'. . . it shone brightly every night for a week." Notice the ghostly ships in the lower border – a sign of things to come.

This section of the Bayeux Tapestry shows the Normans preparing to load their ships. Here they are seen with spears and helmets and an enormous barrel of wine. The Normans had to take all immediate provisions with them.

Part of the Norman fleet crossing the Channel. The ships were small, clinker-built and powered by a large central sail and a rudder. Although some ships have oar holes, none are using oars. In some ships, men and horses are huddled uncomfortably together.

board, their only fear being that they might be left behind", and the Duke, "hot with excitement, bellowed orders to anyone whom he saw lagging and exhorted them all to embark".

By nightfall on the same day, the invasion fleet of some 696 ships was ready to put to sea. After saying hasty prayers of thanks to the patron saint of the harbour, St Valéry, William went aboard his own ship, the *Mora*. Lanterns were hoisted on to the mast of each ship and under cover of darkness the fleet moved out into the Channel, William's ship leading the way. During the night, the ships anchored, and continued crossing in the early morning so that disembarkation could take place in daylight. There is no evidence that the fleet was accompanied by any armed escorts, though William must have feared that the English King, Harold II, might not be far away.

At first light, the Duke awoke to find that the *Mora* was alone on the sea and no other ship, friend or foe, was anywhere to be seen. So as not to alarm his men, William ate a hearty breakfast, washed down with wine, and appeared jovial and relaxed. To his immense relief, the first ships to appear on the horizon were his own, and once reunited, the fleet sailed on towards the Sussex coastline, eventually landing in Pevensey Bay. The voyage was in itself a great achievement; only two ships had been lost in the crossing. One of those contained the official fortune teller, causing William to remark dryly that he could not have been any good if he could not foresee his own death! The other ship came ashore near Romney and all on board were killed by the local inhabitants, an act which they were to pay for later.

Disembarkation

The coastline around Pevensey in the eleventh century was very different from that of today, for the land has now reclaimed much of what were then creeks and mud flats. These provided good natural harbours, but the marshy ground made disembarking difficult. Stepping on to English soil, William met with an unfortunate accident – he slipped and fell flat in the mud! This may not have seemed a good omen but, quick-witted as ever, William turned the situation to his own advantage and, according to Robert Wace, cried: "By God's splendour I have seized the soil of England in both my hands!" In his book the *Roman de Rou*, Wace explains how the disembarkation was achieved: "The archers were the first to land, each with his bow bent and his quiver full of arrows slung at his side . . . . All stood well equipped and in good courage ready for the fight . . . the knights landed next, all armed; with their hauberks on, their shields slung at their necks and their helmets laced." Obviously, William and his men were prepared for immediate battle, but in fact their landing was unopposed. There was no resistance, indeed, no sign of anybody at all.

After an improvised but satisfying meal, William and twenty-five knights rode out to reconnoître the area. The land was so treacherous that they were forced to dismount, take off their heavy armour and return to camp on foot. William distinguished himself by carrying not only his own hauberk, but a companion's as well.

Within the well-preserved remains of the old Roman fort of Anderida, the Normans erected a small wooden castle, protected by a ditch, bank and palisades. It has been suggested that they may even have brought this castle with them, in pieces, ready to erect as soon as they arrived. But because of the unsuitability of the terrain, "the Duke did not long remain in this place [Pevensey] but went away with his men to a port not far distant called Hastings; and there having acquired an appropriate place . . . speedily built a castle of wood. And having burnt the greatest part of his ships (lest any of his followers relying on the hope of returning home should be careless in the design they had undertaken) the Duke . . . anxiously hastened to reduce the surrounding area" (Chronicle of Battle Abbey).

The move to Hastings was another feat of military organization and quite how it was achieved is uncertain. It seems likely that the infantry marched along the coast, using

Pevensey Castle today. On arriving in Pevensey, the Normans built a small castle within the ruins of the old Roman fort of Anderida. After the Conquest the castle was strengthened and used as an administrative centre. Most of the existing remains date from the thirteenth century.

an old pack-horse route, but the rest of the army may well have re-embarked and sailed around the coast to Hastings. Here the invasion force made their camp, and prepared to await the arrival of the English army.

William's plan

Within a few days of arriving in Hastings, William had decided upon a plan which was straightforward and sound. He intended simply to stay put at Hastings and let Harold come to him. To hasten the King's arrival, William ordered the systematic destruction of the surrounding countryside, for he knew that such an act of aggression would enrage Harold and make him react to the Normans' presence more quickly.

In Hastings, William was approached by Robert, son of Guimara, a fellow Norman who was resident in England. Robert came to warn the Duke that Harold had just won an overwhelming victory over the Norwegian King. Rather recklessly, he stated that, compared with Harold's valiant men, William's own troops were nothing more than "a rabble of miserable curs". William's reply was fiery: "If I had only 10,000 men under command of the same temper as the 60,000 I have brought with me, with God to help me, and my own brave troops, I would still not hesitate to march out and destroy him [Harold] and his army." The "60,000" is an extreme example of William of Poitiers' poetic licence and not to be taken seriously!

Harald Hardrada and the Norwegians

So where was King Harold, and why had there been no resistance to either the crossing of the Channel or the landing at Pevensey? The simple answer is that Harold had been the victim of extreme bad luck. A few days before the Normans had landed, he had been forced to lead an army north to Yorkshire, to deal with another invasion – one that appears to have been totally unexpected.

The Norwegian invasion fleet of 300 ships had set sail early in September, under the direction of the King, Harald Hardrada, and in collaboration with Harold's outlawed brother, Tostig. Harald Hardrada believed that he too had a claim to the English throne and intended to do something about it. After ravaging the Cleveland coastline, the Norwegians burnt Scarborough and then sailed up the Ouse to Riccall, just outside York. Here they made their base. On 20th September, the northern earls Edwin and Morcar went out to challenge the Norwegians, but were defeated at the battle of Gate Fulford. Harald Hardrada went on to occupy York, where he was duly proclaimed King.

Within a few days, Harold learned of his countrymen's defeat and had no alternative but to march to York, from London, to help his subjects and secure his own position. With a hastily gathered army he made a spectacular forced march north, arriving in York on the morning of 25th September. The *Anglo-Saxon Chronicle* describes events: "Then came Harold, the King of England, with all his levies . . . to Tadcaster and there drew up his household troops in battle order; and on the Monday he marched through York . . . . Then Harold came up upon them [the Norwegians] unawares beyond the bridge. They joined battle and fierce fighting went on all day." At the end of the day Harold had won a decisive victory and shown himself to be a commander of the highest calibre. The Norwegians suffered shocking losses. Harald Hardrada, Earl Tostig and 7000 men lay dead. Only 24 ships out of the original 300 were needed to take the Norwegian survivors home.

Tradition has it that it was at a feast in York, on 1st October, to celebrate his victory at the Battle of Stamford Bridge, that Harold heard of William's arrival. The messenger, who had ridden the 270 miles from Hastings to York in an astonishingly short time of four days, told Harold that William had landed with an army that was as "numerous as the fish in the sea" (Guy of Amiens). Harold was not impressed and again decided to act with great speed. The *Brevis Relatio*, written anonymously during the early twelfth century, explains Harold's reaction: "He ordered his men to prepare themselves with speed that they might come upon the Normans . . . before they could flee from England; for in his madness, he thought that the Normans would not await him, nor come out to fight against him." The *Brevis* concludes ominously: "But it happened otherwise."

Harold marches south

Harold and the veterans of Stamford Bridge left York on 1st or 2nd October, and marched to London, recruiting members of the local shire levies (militia) on the way. Before entering the capital, Harold paused briefly to offer prayers in Waltham Abbey, a church he had founded in 1060. Here a miracle is said to have occurred: when the King bowed his head towards the crucifix, the figure on the cross is said to have bowed back. All who saw this proclaimed that it was a sign from God that Harold was about to win another victory.

An exterior view of Holy Cross Church, Waltham, which Harold founded in 1060. He stopped here to pray on his way from York to London. In the foreground is a stone which marks the traditional burial place of the King.

The King eventually arrived in London on 6th October and remained for six days, gathering reinforcements and supplies. Early on 12th October, he left London and began the 60-mile march to Sussex. Although Harold, his elite military force, the housecarls, and anyone else who had a horse, rode, the majority of the English army (the fyrd) travelled on foot. By dusk on Friday, 13th, having marched day and night, Harold and the core of his army arrived at the selected rendezvous – Caldbec Hill. Here they made their camp. Foot-weary and exhausted, those who had fought in the north had achieved an incredible march of 270 miles in seven marching days!

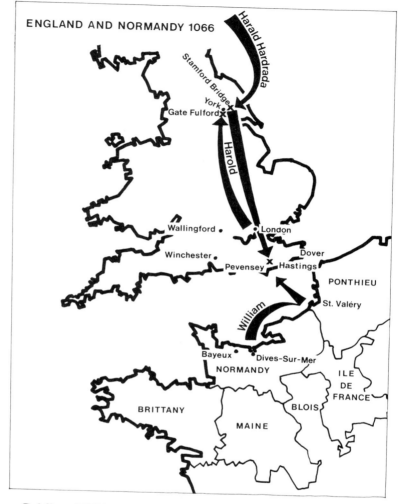

ENGLAND AND NORMANDY 1066

Caldbec Hill had been carefully chosen as a meeting place by Harold, who must have remembered it from when he was in Sussex during the early summer. The hill had many advantages. Firstly, a "hoar apple tree" grew there, an ancient marker of the boundary between the three hundreds (shire divisions) of Catsfield, Ninfield and Baldslow. The hill was thus a familiar local landmark and could be described easily to strangers. Secondly, Caldbec was very close to the objective – Hastings was only seven miles away. Thirdly, the hill was in a strategic position. A minor Roman road ran close to it, and this joined up with the main Rochester to London road, the only route the Normans could take if they wanted to march into the interior and the capital.

Secure in his choice of camp, Harold was able to spend a confident if not restful night. Other shire levies arrived to swell the numbers of his army. Although many were local men, some had come from Somerset and Devon and levies from the North and Midlands had been promised and were expected.

According to Norman writers, who were generally biased against the English, Harold's army spent the night carousing! This can quickly be dismissed as Norman propaganda, aimed at blackening the English reputation, for few of Harold's soldiers would have had the time or energy to so indulge themselves. Robert Wace, writing in the late twelfth century, tells of Harold and his men constructing impressive, wooden fortifications, but archaeologists have since uncovered only a few basic trenches and it is unlikely that Harold would have had time to build anything more elaborate. Instead, preparations were more practical. As soon as a camp had been established, the King sent scouts into the countryside to determine William's exact whereabouts.

Harold's scouts were very efficient and by midnight he knew where to find the enemy. One man reported back with some alarm that many of the Normans appeared to be priests, for "they had the whole face with both lips shaven" (William of Malmesbury). Harold, who was familiar with Norman shaving habits (in England, only the priests were clean-shaven; most men sported moustaches) was able to reassure his men that they would be fighting ordinary soldiers, not clerics. (Nevertheless, many churchmen did fight, Bishop Odo of Bayeux being a prime example).

The enemies' position known, Harold outlined his plan of campaign to his assembled army. He intended to make a surprise attack at dawn, firstly wiping out any foraging parties and then going in to take the main army. His plan relied on the element of surprise and was virtually a repeat of the tactics he had used so effectively nineteen days before at Stamford Bridge. To prevent a Norman retreat homeward, a fleet of 70 ships was already positioning itself in the Channel. Harold also pointed out that the very presence of the English army on Caldbec Hill made a Norman retreat inland impossible.

By the early hours of Saturday, 14th October, English morale was high. Their plan was sound, their position secure and their King a proved capable leader. With the glory of Stamford Bridge fresh in the memory, little remained to be done but clean and sharpen weapons, eat a hasty meal and prepare mentally and physically for the dawn.

Saturday, 14th October: The day of the battle

Dawn: William's preparations

As Harold's men were preparing for battle, a scout arrived in the Norman camp with the disturbing news that the King was not far away – William, too, had excellent scouts. As Harold had hoped, William was taken completely by surprise by the speed with which the English army had marched from London. But he was not a man to sit still and meekly let things happen to him; he would turn the situation to his own advantage. Instead of letting Harold come to him, as he had originally planned, the Duke decided that he would go to the King. He called to arms all the men in his camp – mostly archers and infantrymen, since the majority of the knights were out foraging in what was becoming a severely impoverished countryside. Messengers were quickly sent out to bring back the knights, and scouts were despatched to report on Harold's activities.

While his men prepared themselves, William donned his armour. In his haste, he put on his hauberk back to front. This could have been interpreted as an ominous sign, but, according to William of Poitiers, the Duke "laughed to see it slide, judging it to be pure chance and not a bad augury sent to frighten him". William then attended a short mass conducted by the Bishops Odo of Bayeux and Geoffrey of Coutances. After taking Holy Communion, the Duke hung around his neck some holy relics – the very ones upon which Harold had sworn to be William's vassal.

Shortly before dawn the Norman army assembled into a marching column, which must have been between two and four miles long, depending on how tightly it was formed. The archers and bowmen were placed in the front, the infantrymen in the centre. Taking up the rear were the mounted knights, with William "in the middle surrounded by the elite of his knights, so that he could send orders in all directions by hand signals and shouting" (William of Poitiers). With the banner donated by the Pope fluttering above him, William could feel secure in the belief that his was the honourable and holy course of action, and that Harold was shortly to receive God's judgement of his sins.

At 6.30 on an unusually bright autumn morning, the Norman army wound its way into the green Sussex countryside.

Harold's change of plan

William's decision to call his men to arms was soon reported back to Harold, who, in turn, was forced to change his original plan. Realizing that a surprise attack on the Normans was now out of the question, Harold decided to take advantage of his strong defensive position and to allow William to come to him. However, instead of remaining on Caldbec Hill, the King decided to concentrate his forces on a small ridge half a mile to the south.

The ridge lay in what was then known as Santlache Valley, and was approximately 730 metres long and 135 metres wide. The gentle slope down from the summit ended in boggy ground, which was criss-crossed by eight small streams. Behind the ridge, and to each side of it, lay the densely forested area of the Andredsweald. The strength of Senlac Hill, as it is now known, was its defensive position, for it could only be approached from one direction and then across difficult, marshy ground. To reach the top would involve an arduous clamber, for the incline itself extended for several hundred metres. In short, Senlac was an ideal site from which foot soldiers could conduct a defensive battle against a mounted army.

By first light, Harold's army was preparing to mass on the ridge. This mobilization took several hours, and the fyrd was still assembling when William's army reached Telham Hill, a mile away to the south.

8 am: Telham Hill

At approximately 8 am, the Norman army paused at Telham Hill so that a reconnoître of the area could be made. Here William was met by a member of his advance party, a knight called Vital, who informed the Duke that the English were close. Leading the reconnoître himself, William remarked that in front of him he could see "the forest glitter full of spears" – this was the English army. Rumours spread quickly through the French and Norman ranks about the size and strength of their adversaries, fear and anticipation making most of their guesses wildly extravagant. William of Poitiers acknowledged that "enormous forces of Englishmen had come together from all parts of the country, some through their devotion to Harold, all because of their love for their fatherland, which they were determined to defend against foreign invaders, however wrongly". Guy of Amiens, in his *Carmen de Hastingae Proelio*, written a few years after the battle, gives the number of assembled English as 120,000 – a huge exaggeration, aimed at making the Normans look even more heroic for taking on such a colossal force. In reality, the two sides were evenly matched, with between 7000 and 8000 men each.

At 8.45 am, satisfied with his reconnoître, William ordered his men to move down into the valley and prepare for deployment into battle-lines.

9 am: The Norman deployment

The deployment of the Norman army into formal battle-lines was achieved within full view of the English, on flat land some

Plan of the battlefield.

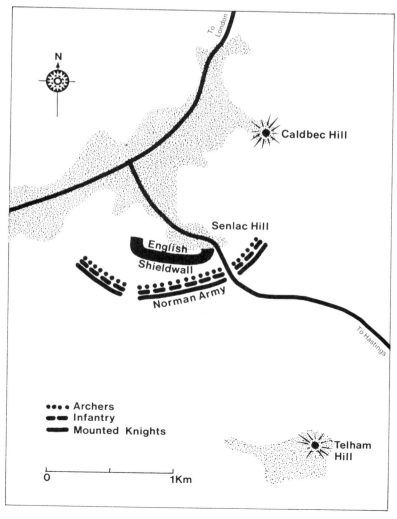

640 metres from the ridge. The eventual formation was a traditional one, parallel to and opposite the enemy. The army was arranged in three distinct divisions: on the left flank were the Poitevins, Manceaux and Bretons, led by Alan Fergeant, Count of Brittany; on the right, Eustace of Boulogne and Roger of Montgomery led the Boulonnais and the men from the Ile de France; while in the centre the Duke commanded the Normans. In all three divisions the formation was the same – archers in the front line, infantrymen behind them, with the mounted knights at the rear.

By 9.30 am, deployment was concluded and William made a morale-boosting pre-battle speech to his men. William of Poitiers' account of the speech is not considered to be a word-for-word account. It was the chroniclers' job to write long, extravagant speeches to show their lord in the most heroic light. In a traditional vein, William of Poitiers has the Duke reminding the French and Normans of their glorious heritage and their national and individual honour, and concluding with the stirring message that "they should all be daring, they must never yield and in less than no time they would rejoice in victory".

Harold's formation

Judging from contemporary accounts, Harold's army was still mobilizing when the Normans came into view. The Anglo-Saxon Chronicle states that: "William came up upon him [Harold] before his army was set in order". There are even veiled hints in the *Carmen* that there may have been a brief skirmish to gain control of the ridge. If this was so, the Normans were quickly and embarrassingly pushed back.

The activities of Harold are well-recorded: "Preparing to meet the enemy, the King mounted the hill and strengthened both his wings with noblemen. On the highest point of the summit, he planted his banner [the fighting man] and he ordered his other standard [the golden dragon of Wessex] to be set up" (Guy of Amiens). On seeing these standards, William realized, possibly for the first time, that Harold was there in person, and he swore that if he were victorious in the forthcoming battle, he would erect an altar on the spot where the King's standards had flown.

The English battle-line was arranged very differently from that of the Normans. The men were grouped "in massed order, the English custom": that is, they were tightly packed

This is a view of the battlefield from William's position and shows the gentle but long incline leading up to the English line. The English shieldwall would have stretched along the entire length of the ridge, the King being in the centre where the abbey now is.

along the length of the small ridge in what was known as a shieldwall. There is controversy about how the shieldwall was formed, but most likely the shields were held so tightly together that they overlapped, affording an excellent defence against such missiles as arrows and stones. To achieve a shieldwall, the men stood sideways, as shown in the Bayeux Tapestry. (After the initial onslaught and when hand-to-hand fighting became inevitable, the shields were probably stuck in the ground and used as a barricade, leaving the men with hands free to fight.) The front line was composed of the King's superior warriors, the housecarls. Harold was in the centre, while both flanks were reinforced with noblemen noted for their military prowess. Somewhere in the front line were the earls Gyrth and Leofwine, Harold's brothers. Behind the housecarls were the more experienced and better-

The Bayeux Tapestry's portrayal of the English shieldwall. The curly line represents the ridge. The English and Normans are shown wearing identical hauberks, and there is one archer without mail.

equipped members of the fyrd, while at the back were the more lowly rank and file, some of whom had never fought before and probably had little idea of the reasons for the battle. Once assembled, the English army was an impressive sight, as it stretched along the length of Senlac Hill, a solid mass, ten to twelve men thick.

10 am: The first attack. "Deux Aie!"

By 10 am, both sides were prepared for battle and stood facing each other – the English high on the ridge, the Normans in the lowland below them. Seizing the initiative, a Norman minstrel unexpectedly galloped towards the English line. "He heartened the men of France and terrified the English, and tossing his sword high, he sported with it. A certain Englishman . . . was fired with ardours proper to a soldier's heart – heedless of life, he sprang forward to meet his death. The mummer, surnamed Taillefer . . . pricked his horse with his spurs; he pierced the Englishman's shield with his keen lance and hewed the head from the prostrate body with his sword. Turning his eyes to his comrades, he displayed this trophy and showed the beginning of the battle favoured them. All rejoiced . . . a tremor ran through brave hearts and at once the men hastened to close shields" (Guy of Amiens). Taillefer went on to kill at least three more men before he himself was slain. Encouraged by such reckless bravery, the Normans made the first move and with braying of trumpets

This is the view which Harold and his men would have had, as they gazed down into the lowland where the Norman army was positioned.

and yells of "Deux Aie!" (God help us!), William's men drew arms.

The Duke's plan was as follows. The archers were to advance to within 150 metres of the English line, fire and inflict as many injuries as possible, so allowing the infantry to move in and hack holes in an already "softened-up" shieldwall. Once enough gaps had been made, the knights were to charge in and annihilate the remainder of the English army. William of Poitiers gives this account of what actually happened: "First the band of archers attacked and from a distance transfixed bodies with their shafts and the crossbowmen destroyed their shields as if by a hailstorm. Now the French attacked the left, the Bretons the right, the Duke with the Normans fought in the centre. The English stood firm on the ground in the closest order. They met missile with missile, sword stroke with sword stroke." By 10.30 am the battle was well under way and being fiercely contested. "The din of the shouting of the Normans on this side and the barbarians on that, could hardly be heard for the clang of their weapons and the groans of the dying." In marked contrast to a modern battle, there was no thunder of tanks, no frightening display of artillery, no acrid black smoke, no gun fire: just human noises and the screams of horses. A mile away from Senlac no one would have known what terrible things were going on in the countryside.

11 am: Retreat and pursuit

By around 11 am, it was becoming increasingly obvious to William that all was not going according to plan. The archers had made little impact on the shieldwall, which was as impressive as ever. Moreover, the bowmen were running out of arrows. In medieval warfare, each side relied upon the return of enemy missiles to replenish its own stock. The English had few archers, and so hardly any arrows were being returned. The infantrymen, when they came in, met with a firm and terrifying response as " . . . the English hurled their javelins and weapons of all sorts; they dealt savage blows with their axes and with stones hafted on handles" (Guy of Amiens). Consequently, when the knights charged up to do their worst, the resistance was still formidable. Suddenly events took a dramatic turn, as William of Poitiers explains: "With great vigour the [English] held those who dare attack them hand to hand and with their swords began to drive them back . . . . The Norman infantry turned in flight, terrified by this savage onslaught, and so did the knights from Brittany and the other auxiliaries on the left flank. Almost the whole line of the Duke fell back."

For the most part, this retreat was accomplished in an orderly fashion, the Normans moving off with "their shields covering their backs". However, the Bretons, particularly their inexperienced young squires, fled in considerable disarray: the squires' horses bolted out of control into the marshy ground at the side of the battlefield. Then something totally unexpected happened. A large section of the fyrd left its position on the ridge and rushed down into the valley in pursuit of the fleeing Bretons. The French chroniclers tend to dismiss this as the action of a disobedient and disorganized rabble, but the resulting panic and confusion in the Norman army suggest that the English move was a deliberate counter-attack authorised by Harold.

At the same time, and to add to the chaos, a rumour spread through the Norman army that William had been killed. For a moment the future looked grim for the Normans and it seemed that Harold was about to gain another victory. However, William was merely unhorsed, and upon hearing of his own supposed death, mounted another horse and made a highly effective gesture. Throwing back the nasal of his helmet, he brandished his mace at his fleeing men and roared, "Look at me! I am still alive! What lunacy makes you turn in flight? What retreat is open to you if you run? They will drive

The Bayeux Tapestry shows William lifting his visor to show his retreating men that he is still alive. The knight on the right is carrying the papal banner.

you on and slaughter you! You have it in your power to cut them down like a flock of sheep! You are giving up victory and fame which could last forever. If you keep on not a single one of you will escape" (William of Poitiers).

Hearing this, the retreating knights reorganized themselves under William's command and, joining forces with a previously unused section of the cavalry, wheeled their horses around and charged back to encircle their pursuers. They "wiped them out in a moment so there was not a single survivor".

A pause

After the first, exhausting phase of the battle, a lengthy pause was inevitable, as both sides re-formed, recovered and reconsidered the situation. The Normans regrouped in the valley, while the English shieldwall was strengthened. Missiles were retrieved and any food and water available were gratefully consumed.

Noon: The second attack. "Out! Out"

Harold's plan did not alter. The shieldwall re-formed and waited for the second onslaught. William, however, decided to try a change in tactics and ordered a general attack to be made by the mounted knights. Led by the Duke, Bishop Odo of Bayeux and Robert, son of Roger of Beaumont, the knights trotted their horses up the hill towards the English. To imagine a dramatic cavalry charge reminiscent of the Light Brigade is wrong, for the terrain was difficult and the horses were small and stocky, and so their pace would have been rather slow. Again the knights were received with a ferocious barrage as the English, yelling their battle-cries of "God Almighty!" and "Out! Out!", pelted the Normans with everything from stones to axes. During this period of heavy fighting Harold's two brothers, Gyrth and Leofwine, were killed. According to Guy of Amiens, renowned more for his poetic writing than for his accuracy, Gyrth was killed by William, who mistook him for his elder brother: "Harold's brother, Gyrth by name . . . was undaunted by the face of the lion [William]; poising a javelin, he hurled it from afar with a strong arm. The flying weapon wounded the body of the horse and forced the Duke to fight on foot; but reduced to a foot soldier he fought yet better, for he rushed upon the young man like a snarling lion. Hewing him limb from limb, he shouted to him 'take the crown you have earned from us!' "

In spite of William's personal bravery and direction, the French and Flemish knights were once again pushed back by the English and appeared to retreat in panic. This time there was a difference. According to several chroniclers, this retreat was a deliberate strategy designed to lure a section of the fyrd down from the ridge in order to massacre them. If this was so, it worked. "The Normans . . . realized that they could never overcome the vast army of their enemies, all fighting as one man, unless they were prepared for heavy losses. They therefore withdrew, deliberately pretending to turn in flight. They were mindful of the fact that only a short time before their retreat had been turned into success . . . . As happened on the previous occasion, some thousand or more English rushed boldly forward, thinking to harass those who were running away. Suddenly the Normans turned their horses, cut off the force which was pursuing them and massacred them to the last man" (William of Poitiers).

By medieval standards, the battle was lasting for a

considerable time, for it was now well into the afternoon. Men and horses were becoming exhausted and took advantage of a brief lull in the fighting to recover strength and regain weapons.

Late afternoon: The third attack.
"The strength of Hercules"

The English were becoming worryingly reduced in number and demoralized by their two disastrous attempts to follow up an advantage. Although contingents from the North and Midlands had been promised, they had not arrived – probably because their own numbers were so severely depleted after the battles of Gate Fulford and Stamford Bridge, rather than as a result of treachery, as has sometimes been suggested. Reinforcements did continue to trickle into Harold's army during the day, but not in sufficient numbers to make any real impression. Consequently, all ranks of the fyrd drew in closer to the royal standards, which were still flying on the summit of the ridge.

Meanwhile the ever-inventive William planned his third assault. This time he decided to try a combined attack by all three divisions of his army – archers, infantrymen and knights. The archers were ordered to use high-angle fire, which meant aiming high into the sky so that their arrows would go over the heads of the men in the English front line and land on the less well-protected soldiers at the back. Also, with the archers aiming high, the Norman infantry could advance simultaneously, without fear of being hit by the arrows of their own side – normally a real risk. The knights, many of whom were now unhorsed, were ordered to advance at the same time as the infantry. Attacks were to be made in a three-pronged offensive, aiming at the centre and at each flank of the shieldwall.

The attack was duly launched and, as usual, William was in the thick of it. His mere presence was enough for some Englishmen, if Guy of Amiens is to be believed: "At the sight of this wonderful and redoubtable knight many enemies lost heart before they received a scratch." It is more likely that they just fainted from exhaustion and lack of food. It was not only his opponents who were terrified by the Duke; some of his own men were also plainly in awe of him. Having lost yet another horse, William was fighting on foot, "with the strength of Hercules", when he saw " . . . a knight of Maine riding through the slaughter . . . he signed to him with a sword dyed with brains and gore to come to his aid. But he [the knight] refused to save him . . . terrified of his own death as a hare before a hound. The Duke . . . suddenly turned upon him, seizing him furiously by the nasal . . . tumbled him head over heels to the ground, and rushed to mount the horse thus left to him" (Guy of Amiens). William was unhorsed three times in rapid succession during this part of the battle, and by the third time he was raging: " . . . seeing the author of the crime lurking at a distance in the press, he rushed forthwith to destroy him. Cutting through his groin with a thrust of his right hand and a merciless sword stroke with his left, he spilt his entrails on the ground." Although the pro-Norman chroniclers do not admit the fact, their accounts suggest that this was a very dangerous period for the Normans, since control appeared to be slipping from William's hands and his own men had become confused and frightened. The Duke was eventually helped out of his perilous situation by Eustace of Boulogne, who, seeing William's plight, dismounted and went to fight with him on foot. A fearsome team, they hacked their way through the English.

Not so much is recorded about Harold's activities, although William of Malmesbury, writing in the early twelfth century, tells that the King also performed heroic feats: "Harold hit out repeatedly at every enemy who came within striking distance, dashing horse and horsemen to the ground with a single blow, so that none came near him without paying dearly for it."

As William of Poiters points out, "the fighting was most unusual, for one side continued the attack in a series of charges and individual assaults, while the other stood firmly rooted to the ground". The immobility of the English was to prove a fatal flaw in their tactics, but their resistance and courage were still strong, even at this late stage in the afternoon. However, their losses were high: "The dead as they tumbled to the ground showed more sign of motion than the living. The serried mass of their companions prevented those who were lightly wounded from withdrawing, so tightly were they grouped together." The Normans, although also seriously weakened, were undaunted and still in high spirits, spurred on by the enthusiastic and untiring leadership of the Duke: "His foot soldiers took new courage when they saw him fighting on foot. Some, who were weak from loss of blood, leaned on their shields and fought on manfully; others, who could do no more, shouted to their companions, encouraging them to follow where the Duke led."

Late afternoon: The death of Harold

As the light began to fade, William ordered simultaneous attacks by his mounted knights on the remaining English on the right and left flanks of the shieldwall. The combined pressure was successful and threw the fyrd, by now exhausted, into confusion. At about this time "an arrow that had been thus shot towards the sky [i.e. high] struck Harold above the eye, and put one of his eyes out. In his wrath, he drew it out and threw it away, breaking it with his hands; and the pain to his head was so great that he leaned upon his shield" (Robert Wace). Harold's injury did not go unnoticed, for someone, possibly William, ordered a group of knights to go in and finish him off. Henry of Huntingdon said that twenty knights attempted to get past the still loyal housecarls and, as they attacked, at least half of these knights were killed. In the end, four knights, named by Guy of Amiens as Eustace of Boulogne, a son of Guy of Ponthieu, Hugh

It is now believed that both the figure with the arrow in his eye and the one being slashed by a mounted knight represent Harold. This manner of death is born out by several of the chroniclers. Notice the pillaging depicted in the lower border.

Gifford and Geoffrey of Montfort, quickly dealt with the injured King: " . . . these four between them encompassed the death of the King. . . . With the point of his lance, the first pierced Harold's shield and then penetrated his chest, drenching the ground with his blood . . . with his sword, the second cut off his head . . . the third disembowelled him with his javelin. The fourth hacked his leg off at the thigh and hurled it far away. Struck down in this way, his dead body lay on the ground" (Guy of Amiens). William of Malmesbury bears out this story, without going into quite so much gory detail, and simply states that Harold was first struck in the eye by an arrow and then hacked in the thigh by a nameless soldier, for which "cowardly and shameful act" he was subsequently expelled from the army. The Bayeux Tapestry gives visual confirmation of this story, but the other most reliable source, William of Poitiers, is oddly silent about the details of Harold's death, which suggests that there was something less than glorious in the manner in which he was killed.

5 pm: Twilight

Reports of Harold's death caused even more confusion and despair among the ranks of the fyrd, though the housecarls fought on doggedly around the still-flying royal standards. At around 5 pm, with darkness rapidly falling, "the English, after having persisted bravely in their fight the whole day, on learning that their king was dead, began to tremble for their safety; and under cover of the night, they turned away and sought safety in flight" (William of Jumièges).

Within an hour, the Normans were in possession of the ridge, but William was still not content and ordered a pursuit of the fleeing soldiers. "The English turned in flight and made off at full speed, some on horses which they had seized, others on foot along the trackways, most of them through the pathless desert. Bathed in their own blood, they struggled to escape, while others dragged themselves to their feet but could not walk a step . . . . Although the country was unknown to them, the Normans pursued them relentlessly, cutting down the fugitives from behind and putting the finishing touches to the victory which they had won. Their horses' hooves took a last toll of the corpses, as they rode over them where they lay" (William of Poitiers). Guy of Amiens says that this pursuit went on throughout the night and into the next day, but that is most unlikely.

This scene from the Bayeux Tapestry has been interpreted by some historians as representing the Malfosse incident, although it does not appear in the correct place, chronologically, for this. The English are clearly on a hillock and the mounted Normans appear to be falling into some kind of ravine. The English are all unmailed and sport moustaches.

Nightfall: The Malfosse

One group of pursuing Normans, led by Eustace of Boulogne, rode northwards in the direction of Caldbec Hill. As they galloped through the woods, they saw in front of them a group of housecarls, jeering and shouting from a small hillock. The Normans charged towards them, unaware that the grass concealed a hidden ditch. William of Jumièges, writing in 1071, gives this account of the disaster that befell them: "The Normans seeing the English escaping pursued them obstinately . . . but to their own detriment, for the long grass hid from them an old ditch into which the Normans were suddenly precipitated, and into it they fell with their horses and their armour, killing one another as they fell one on top of the other, without any warning." Once in the ditch, named by the Chronicle of Battle Abbey as the Malfosse (evil ditch), the Normans were pelted with missiles by the still defiant English. Eustace escaped the fate of many of his companions and hurried back to tell William what had happened. True to character, the Duke refused to be beaten by even this insignificant encounter and ordered Eustace and his remaining men to turn round and go back. As they approached the area, Eustace was struck down by a hiding housecarl and carried from the field, wounded but not killed. Enraged, William summoned his men and "advanced against the enemy and flung them to the ground". After more savage fighting, the Duke took control of the situation and the battle ended.

Returning to the battlefield, the Duke gave "thanks to God, and in his pride, ordered his gonfanon [banner] to be brought and set up on high where the King's standards had stood . . . and he ordered his tent to be raised on this spot among the dead, and had his meat brought thither, and his supper prepared there . . . . And he ate and drank among the dead, and made his bed that night upon the field" (Robert Wace).

So ended one of the most important battles ever to be fought on English soil – a battle which was to earn William, Duke of Normandy, the title of "the Conqueror", and which was to have immediate and far-reaching effects on England and her people.

Making sure of victory

Sunday, 15th October, was a grim day. Although the Normans had won an important victory, their future was by no means certain. How would they be received in this foreign land? Was another army being assembled in haste to challenge them? The Duke had won the battle, but would he be recognized as King? However, on the day after the battle, there were more pressing things to attend to.

The most important was the burial of the dead. Senlac Hill was covered with bodies, both Norman and English. It has been estimated that 30 per cent of the Norman army lost their lives, while the English probably suffered greater losses. The King lay dead, as did his two brothers and the "flower of English youth and nobility" (Orderic Vitalis). Where the Normans buried their dead is unknown, for, as yet, no mass graves have been identified. As for the English, local people came to look for the bodies of their menfolk, but the majority were "left to be eaten by the worms and wolves, birds and dogs". The dead were stripped of their mail, weapons and valuables, and, judging from the Bayeux Tapestry, this looting had begun even before the battle ended.

The burial of Harold

What happened to the body of Harold has always been a mystery. Explanations tend to come from the realms of folk-lore rather than truth. By all accounts, the King's body was so badly mutilated that it could be identified only by his "hand-fast" wife Edith Svenngals. (They had been married in a Danish rather than a church ceremony.) Once it was found, the corpse was William's responsibility and he did not seem to know quite what to do with it. Harold's mother came to the Duke and pleaded with him to give her the body of her son, even offering to pay Harold's weight in gold. Embarrassed and disgusted by such an idea, William refused and instead gave the body into the care of one of his servants, William Malet. Guy of Amiens tells a strange story: he says that William carried the dead King, shrouded in royal purple, to a cliff where he was buried overlooking the sea. A stone bearing the following epitaph marked the spot: "By the Duke's command O Harold you rest here a king, that you may still be guardian of the sea and shore". William then proclaimed himself King and symbolically distributed alms to the local poor. This has been interpreted as a pagan burial, similar to the old Viking ceremonies; but this is a controversial interpretation. It is unlikely that such a pious Christian as William would perform such a rite. The most fanciful explanation of Harold's "disappearance" was that he had not been killed at all but had escaped to the Continent. In this version of events he ultimately returned to England and ended his days as a hermit in Chester! Whatever actually happened to his corpse, the King's final resting place has always been considered to be Waltham Abbey, the church which he had founded in 1060.

True to the promise made on Telham Hill, William carefully marked the spot where Harold's standards had been set up, and in 1076 the Abbaye de la Bataille was founded on the ridge, its altar in the place occupied by the King during the battle. As for the royal standards themselves, William sent one which was "sumptuously embroidered in gold and precious stones and represented the form of the fighting man" to the Pope, as proof of his success and a token of his gratitude for the Pope's support.

True to his word, William founded an abbey on the ridge. Little remains of the original abbey, but the central blocked-up window dates from the Norman period.

This memorial stone marks the spot where Harold is believed to have died. The inscription on the stone reads: "The traditional site of the high altar of Battle Abbey founded to commemorate the victory of Duke William on 14 October 1066. The high altar was placed to mark the spot where King Harold died." This photograph was taken a few days after the anniversary of the battle, hence the flowers.

16th-30th October

William's forces were alert and daily expected the arrival of another English army. But nothing happened: no army, no messages, no submissions; just an ominous silence. The future for the Normans looked bleak, for they were seriously reduced in numbers, provisions were very low and the winter was drawing in. On 16th October the army withdrew to Hastings and the security of the camp there. After a week in Hastings, with still no sign of the English, William moved to Dover, where he was expecting reinforcements to arrive from Normandy. The Normans' route from Hastings to Dover is easily discernible from entries in the Domesday Book, compiled over twenty years later, for the villages they passed through are all recorded as being "wasta". The one to suffer most was Romney, whose people had killed the crew of a shipwrecked Norman vessel.

William's entry into Dover was unopposed but unwelcome. Much of the town was set on fire, and looting and plundering took place, against William's orders and to his fury. In Dover, news did begin to filter through, but it was not good. William

Little remains of Hastings Castle, high on the cliff, the second to be built by William on his arrival in England.

learned that Edgar Aethling, grandson of an earlier King, Edmund Ironside (reigned 1016), was being put forward as Harold's successor, and that London was preparing an armed resistance to the Normans. However, the awaited reinforcements arrived from Normandy, and Dover was properly organized as a garrison town.

30th October to 25th December

After eight days in Dover, William decided upon a plan of positive action. His ultimate goal was obviously the capital, London, and it appears that he was expecting a tough fight, for plans were drawn up involving the use of battering rams and siege castles. Firstly, the Duke marched to Canterbury, the ecclesiastical capital, and here, on 31st October, the men of Kent flocked to offer their submissions, "like flies settling upon a wound" (Guy of Amiens). Early in November, a contingent of the army was sent to Southwark, just outside London, which it razed to the ground in an act of deliberate terrorism. Simultaneously, William and the rest of the army moved on to Winchester, the old capital and seat of the treasury. Here William received the submission of Harold's sister, Edith, widow of the previous King, Edward the Confessor. Meanwhile the section of the army near London branched out and began a slow, menacing encircling of the capital, blocking off all the main routes into it. This worked extremely well and at Wallingford the Duke received the first important submission – that of Stigand, Archbishop of Canterbury. A fortnight later at Berkhamsted, Edgar Aethling, Ealdred, Archbishop of York, and the earls Edwin and Morcar came to submit to the Duke and offer him the crown. As a result of extremely clever tactics, William was therefore able to enter London as an invited guest rather than an aggressor. He was duly crowned on Christmas Day and, for better or worse, England had her first Norman King.

This is a page from a thirteenth-century manuscript. The initial drawing shows the coronation of William. The drawing in the right-hand margin is of Battle Abbey.

THE INVESTIGATION

Why did the Normans invade England?

The Norman invasion of England in 1066 was the last successful invasion of the country, and the only one which has earned the title of The Conquest. The first question to ask is why a smaller, comparatively new state decided to take on a larger, better-established power? The simple answer to what is a very complicated question is that William, Duke of Normandy, believed that Harold Godwinson, Earl of Wessex, had stolen what should rightfully have come to him – the throne of England. How justifiable was William's anger and his subsequent action?

The death of Edward the Confessor

On 5th January, 1066, King Edward the Confessor was dying. He had reigned for twenty-four years, was an old man and, most significantly, was childless. According to the *Vita Aedwardi Regis*, written anonymously in 1100, the King on his deathbed "pointed with his hand towards Harold, the man whom he had brought up at his court and whom he looked upon as a brother" and said: "I commend my wife to your care and with her my whole kingdom". The following day, Edward was buried in the newly consecrated Westminster Abbey, and the ceremony was shortly followed by the crowning of the new King, Harold II. Harold's coronation was conducted by Stigand, Archbishop of Canterbury, and was favourably received by the Witan, England's chief advisory council, and the people as a whole.

Harold's claim to the throne

Harold had no blood connection with the English royal family, but in the eleventh century royal blood, though desirable, was not an essential requirement for kingship. Nor was primogeniture – inheritance by the oldest son – an established practice, though the sons of kings obviously stood a good chance of succeeding their fathers. More important were a man's suitability for kingship, and his acceptance by

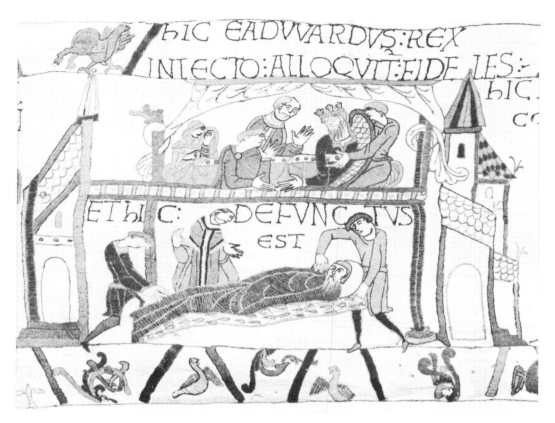

hIC EADWARDVS:REX
INTECTO:ALLOQVIT:FIDE LES:
hIC.
CC

ET hI C: ☩ DEFVNC TVS
EST

The Bayeux Tapestry's portrayal of the death of Edward the Confessor is respectful. As he gives his kingdom into Harold's care, his wife Edith, Archbishop Stigand and an attendant look on.

other powerful magnates. Harold had shown himself to be entirely suitable. He was the second son of the most powerful earl in the kingdom, Earl Godwin, who, with his numerous sons, had controlled most of the earldoms in England. On his father's death in 1053, Harold had inherited his title and his power and, for the next twelve years, was virtual ruler of the whole country, or "subregulus" as Florence of Worcester called him, for Edward had long since bowed to the dominance of the Godwins and turned his attention to religious affairs. Harold appears to have been highly thought of, having shown himself through his military campaigns and statesmanship, to be an excellent leader of men. Above all, he was English and therefore accepted by other Englishmen. Harold Godwinson was thus the most likely candidate to succeed Edward, and his deathbed nomination was both traditional and acceptable. There was one serious problem, however. During his lifetime, Edward had nominated someone else to succeed him, and that someone else was William, Duke of Normandy.

William's claim to the throne

William, and probably most of Europe, fully expected that he would succeed Edward on the English throne. When the news arrived across the Channel that Harold had been not only nominated but crowned, William was at first astonished and then outraged – not without cause. Unlike Harold, the Duke could claim a family connection with the English royal line: his great aunt, Emma of Normandy, had been married to two Kings of England, Ethelred II (978-1013) and Cnut (1016-35). But this point was insignificant compared with what William believed to have been a binding agreement made between himself and Edward. In 1051, William had visited England as a guest of the King and, during this stay, Edward had apparently nominated the Duke as his successor. According to French sources, this promise was reinforced in 1064 when Edward sent Harold to Normandy, for the express purpose of sealing the agreement. According to William of Poitiers, while in Normandy, Harold swore to be William's vassal and promised to "confirm William in his succession to the throne of England". Harold also promised to fortify Dover for the Duke's use, and there are hints that he may have promised to marry one of William's daughters. What made these oaths doubly binding was that they were sworn on holy relics, probably in Bayeux Cathedral. To break such oaths would be not only dishonourable but also perjury – a mortal sin.

Genealogical tree.

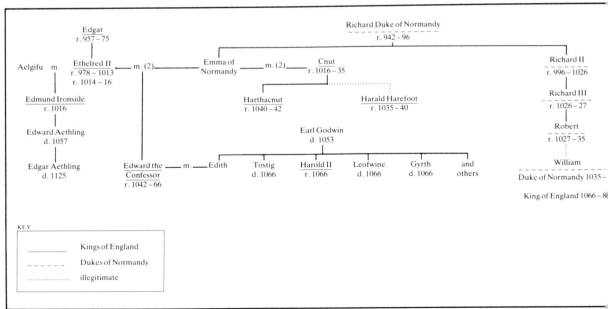

KEY

———————	Kings of England
– – – – –	Dukes of Normandy
....	illegitimate

Did these oaths and agreements exist?

That some sort of agreement was made in 1051 appears certain. From William's point of view it was obviously binding, but Edward's attitude is more difficult to assess. Hakon and Wulfnoth (Harold's nephew and brother) were sent back with William to live as honourable exiles in Normandy – and this suggests that both sides considered the agreement to be serious. But in 1057 Edward invited Edward Aethling, son of Edmund Ironside (r1016), to return to England from exile in Hungary. Edward's invitation to this prince to attend his court suggests that he intended to make him his heir. (In the event the prince died shortly after his arrival in England.) Had Edward's aim been merely to give William a vague promise, in order to keep on amicable terms with him?

The 1064 incident is also very puzzling. The Bayeux Tapestry shows the whole episode in great detail, but it is important to remember that this was a French interpretation of the facts, and one designed to show the victors in the most favourable light. The series of events depicted is as follows: Edward sends Harold to Normandy, but he is blown off course and lands in the territory of the Count of Ponthieu, who makes him his prisoner. William hears of the capture and orders Harold's release. Harold and William go on several campaigns together, William eventually knighting Harold for his bravery. The oath-swearing which follows is clearly shown, though Harold looks very disgruntled throughout,

The Bayeux Tapestry's depiction of the oath-swearing in 1064. William is evidently in control. The reliquaries on which Harold took the oath came from Bayeux Cathedral and contained saints' bones.

and William has a definite air of smugness. Harold is finally allowed home, bearing gifts and taking with him one of the hostages, Hakon. The English chroniclers say nothing of all this, except for one who suggests that Harold simply went on a fishing expedition in the Channel, was shipwrecked off the French coast and captured by the Count of Ponthieu.

So what is the most likely explanation for these obscure events? That an oath was taken in 1064 seems certain; what Harold swore to is less clear. Any promises he made may well have been simply to ensure that he had a safe passage home. (All the scenes in the Tapestry give the distinct impression that Harold was being kept as a distinguished prisoner.) Once back in England, away from William's control, Harold accepted the crown, considering his nomination by Edward on his deathbed more binding than promises made under duress to the Duke. The speed with which Harold was crowned suggests that he was uneasy as to how news of his action might be received by William and others.

Other claimants William and Harold were not the only claimants to the English throne. There were several other candidates, all with reasonably good claims. The most legitimate was Edgar Aethling, grandson of Edmund Ironside and the last descendant of the great King Alfred and the Wessex dynasty that had united England. Edgar's claim was never seriously considered, except briefly after the Conquest, because he was still a child. Two other men believed themselves to have strong claims. Swein, King of Denmark, was the grandson of Swein Forkbeard, King of England in 1013-14, and although he made no serious attempt to claim the throne in 1066, he was an active threat during the early years of William's reign. The final candidate was also a Scandinavian. Harald Hardrada, King of Norway, based his claim on a treaty made between his father, Magnus, and Harthacnut, King of England, 1040-42, in which Harthacnut promised the throne to Magnus, or his successors. Harald was prepared to take action, as has already been seen.

Old disputes William also used old disputes between England and Normandy as excuses for invasion. In 1036, Alfred, the brother of Edward (later the Confessor), had been invited out of his exile in Normandy by the then King of England, Harold Harefoot (r1035-40). While in England, Alfred, apparently at the command of Earl Godwin and with the knowledge of the King, was brutally blinded and eventually died from this.

Edward, who was still in exile in Normandy, and William were outraged and swore revenge on the Godwins. William now added this old grievance against the Godwins to his list of complaints against Harold, even though Harold had been only seven years old when the incident occurred.

The final cause of annoyance, as far as William was concerned, was the English Church – in particular, Stigand, Archbishop of Canterbury. In 1052, the newly appointed Robert of Jumièges, a Norman, had been ousted from the archbishopric of Canterbury, in favour of the English Stigand. Stigand had been excommunicated by the Pope and was not recognized as being the true archbishop, since Jumièges was still alive. The fact that Harold was eventually crowned by Stigand made the whole ceremony, in Norman eyes, a sham.

Was a Norman invasion inevitable?

During the eleventh century, Europe was quite different from what it is today. States were not nations in the modern sense, and their rulers had only very limited powers. France was a recognized country ruled over by a King, but within French territory there were many smaller duchies and counties, each with its own duke, baron or count. Although owing nominal allegiance to the King, these nobles were fiercely independent and almost continually engaged in war against one another.

Normandy was one such area. In 911, by the Treaty of St Clair sur Epte, Charles the Simple, King of France, granted a portion of land to the Norwegian Rollo in order to keep the Viking quiet. This area eventually became known as Normandy, land of the Northmen. A maritime region, it had 160 miles of coastline and stretched from Mont St Michel in the west to Tréport in the east. Thanks to a succession of strong rulers, combined with economic and agrarian prosperity, the duchy flourished and by the eleventh century was enjoying a period of territorial expansion. Wherever there was action there were Normans and by 1066 they had established themselves in several different countries including Spain, Sicily and mainland Italy. Their Scandinavian characteristics had disappeared, and they had become completely French, in language, customs and religion. Society was feudal, centred around the elite group – the knights – who were feared and respected throughout Europe. The Norman church was advanced and influential, but culturally Normandy was not as sophisticated as England, and it is best thought of as a developing country rather than an established one.

By comparison, England was an old-established country whose roots went back to the fifth century. It was well on the way to unification, although there was still a definite distinction between the Scandinavian north and the Anglo-Saxon south. By the eleventh century central government was strong, presided over by a "God-anointed" King, who enjoyed more power than his European counterparts, and an advisory council, the Witan. England also had a complex and efficient system of local government, all of which Normandy lacked. The economy was prosperous, backed up by a strong currency, and trade flourished. Unlike Normandy, England had no knights, but a local and national army was available through the shire levies (fyrd). During its six hundred years of existence England had developed a rich cultural heritage and was renowned for achievements in learning, art and literature. An ancient and wealthy country, England had one weakness. The Church, once so vital, had by the mid-eleventh century fallen into decline and showed little of the piety or zeal of its Norman counterpart.

***The Anglo-Norman
background***

During the reign of Ethelred the Unready (978-1016), diplomatic relations between England and Normandy became important. In 1007, Emma, sister of Duke Richard of Normandy, married King Ethelred. Emma was a formidable and influential woman and, through her, Norman interests were fostered. She brought with her to England her many Norman friends and servants, and encouraged the appointment of Normans to office. When the Danes invaded in 1013, she sent her three children, Alfred, Edward and Godgifu, to Normandy for safe-keeping. After the death of Ethelred, she married the new Danish King, Cnut (1016-35), and relations between England and Normandy remained good until the murder of Alfred in 1036.

Anxious to make amends, the next King, Harthacnut (1040-42), invited Edward (later known as the Confessor) to return to England and nominated the prince as his heir. By this time, Edward was pretty well "Normanized": he had spent most of his youth and young manhood in Normandy, spoke French as his first language and had adapted readily to French customs. When he became King in 1042, he introduced many of his Norman friends and advisers into his court. Although there was no conscious policy of Normanization, Edward's pro-French attitude was highly unpopular in some quarters – especially among the Godwin family.

The rise of the Godwins dominated English politics from the reign of Cnut until the death of Harold. Godwin, Earl of Wessex, became powerful under the patronage of Cnut, and by Edward's reign was the most influential man in the kingdom, after the King. He and his numerous sons occupied most of the earldoms in the country and in 1045 his daughter, Edith, married the King. It seems likely that Edward resented the domineering earl and tried to counteract his influence by surrounding himself with his Norman friends. This was greatly resented by Godwin and in 1051 matters came to a head. At Dover, Eustace of Boulogne, the King's brother-in-law, was involved in a brawl during which several of his men were killed. To punish the people of Dover for having offended his guest, Edward ordered Godwin to burn the town, Dover being in Godwin's earldom. Godwin refused and took up arms against his King, but he backed down at the last moment and accepted exile for himself and his family.

With the Godwins out of the way, Edward invited William to England, and it was during this period that he nominated the Duke as his successor. The next year, however, the Godwins came back and an anti-Norman policy was embarked upon. Many Normans were ousted from office, one of the most notable casualties being Robert of Jumièges, Archbishop of Canterbury, who, according to the Anglo-Saxon Chronicle was "declared utterly an outlaw, and all Frenchmen too, because they were most responsible for the disagreement between Earl Godwin and the King". Jumièges was replaced by the notorious Stigand – who was excommunicated by the Pope for replacing an archbishop who was still alive.

Was a Norman King inevitable?

Current thinking suggests that England was destined to have a Norman King on the death of Edward. An Anglo-Norman friendship had flourished for seventy years and through an agreement in 1052, reinforced by an oath of 1064, William had been assured of a smooth succession. It was only the intervention of Harold Godwinson that made a military conquest necessary. But although the English were familiar with the Normans, there is no evidence that they liked them. Would William have been accepted readily by the English if Harold had not intervened? Would the Witan have nominated another Englishman to be King if Harold had been unwilling to break his oath – Gyrth or Leofwine, for example? Would Harald Hardrada have been more acceptable than William? Countless questions, no positive answers, but much food for thought!

Why did the English lose?

One would not have expected the English to lose the battle, for they had most of the obvious advantages. Firstly, England was the larger, richer and more densely populated country. (Normandy was only the size of the earldom of Wessex.) Secondly, the King was an excellent military leader and his fighting force, the housecarls, was recognized as the best infantry in Europe. Thirdly, the English were fighting on home ground and in the after-glow of their victory at Stamford Bridge. The Normans faced a daunting task, which many of William's advisers had called impossible. William had actually to build a fleet to ferry his men, horses and equipment over the Channel, and once in England he was in largely unknown and definitely hostile territory. He knew he would have to fight, but he had no idea of the strength of the resistance, of how many battles it would take to achieve his end. It was also getting late in the year and unless a speedy victory was obtained, his men would suffer from cold and hunger. Psychologically, William had two advantages: firstly, he and his men had not so much to lose but much more to gain; and secondly, he firmly believed that his cause was just and that God would show him to be the victor.

The non-favourites won. How can this be accounted for?

Early preparations　William's preparations were immediate and thorough. Almost as soon as he heard that Harold had been crowned, he decided that an invasion was his only possible course of action. When the Duke confided his plan to his advisers, they told him he was being foolhardy and unrealistic, but when they realized that he was serious, they urged him to consult his barons, without whose support the enterprise could have gone no further. Accordingly, in April, a conference was held in Lillebonne, where the general reaction was that invasion was impossible. Undaunted and by now determined to go ahead at all costs, William then consulted each baron individually and, by fair means or foul, persuaded each to change his mind. His powers of persuasion were evidently considerable, for all but one then agreed to send either men or ships, though few promised to participate in person. The only man to refuse to support William was Conan of Brittany, who died in mysterious circumstances a few days later – his bridle and hunting horn had been dipped in poison.

William also made other shrewd arrangements and, in particular, ensured that all the major Continental powers knew of his plan, and either supported it, or promised not to invade Normandy while he was away. The most significant support came from an unexpected quarter – the Pope. Lanfranc, Prior of Bec in Normandy, suggested that William should ask for a papal blessing, on the grounds that Harold had not been crowned by a member of the Church. (Stigand had been excommunicated in 1052.) The Archdeacon of Lisieux was duly dispatched to Rome and returned with Pope Alexander II's blessing, a papal banner and a ring said to contain some hair and a tooth belonging to St Peter. Thus equipped, William's campaign gained much respectability, for Harold and all his supporters were excommunicated, and William now claimed that his was a holy crusade to relieve England of an ungodly ruler. Soon recruits began to pour into Normandy, many from Brittany, Aquitaine, Flanders and Anjou. Mercenaries were also attracted by William's enterprise, hoping for wealth and fame.

William's preparations were therefore thorough. Harold's were less so and concentrated only on ensuring support in England. Any opposition to his succession was most likely to come from the north, since the two northern earls were not part of the Godwin family. Harold therefore travelled to York within a few weeks of his coronation. Here he received the official submissions of the earls Edwin and Morcar and, as an added precaution, married their sister, Edith. Harold made no attempt to secure Continental support, nor to justify himself against Duke William's accusations.

Preparations: military

In his military preparations, Harold was more thorough. By May, the fyrd had been called out and local levies were positioned at strategic points along the south coast. The fleet was sent into the Channel, and Harold himself kept an eye on things from the Isle of Wight. Many places were fortified and garrisoned, and an efficient look-out system was organized. In effect, the King kept a large number of the fyrd and fleet fed, watered and occupied for nearly four months, a considerable achievement in management.

On the other side of the water, preparations were also extensive. By the early spring, an army of shipwrights, carpenters and smiths had descended on the Norman harbours and an orgy of shipbuilding got under way. The Bayeux Tapestry is invaluable for showing how the fleet of 696 ships was constructed and provided for. By 12th August the shipbuilding was completed and the fleet gathered at the port of Dives-sur-Mer, waiting for a southerly wind to take it to England. (William, too, had to keep his men content for a considerable period.) After a long month of waiting, the fleet moved 100 miles up the coast, to St-Valéry-sur-Somme, where it was further delayed by "contrary winds". On 27th September the fleet was at last able to sail.

Some historians have said that it was pure chance that William landed at Pevensey, but this underestimates the Duke. Nothing he did was a matter of chance; everything was calculated down to the smallest details. Pevensey was an obvious choice as it was close to St-Valéry, was near Harold's own manor at Bosham and was also close to a Norman settlement. Queen Emma had given some land near Winchelsea to a group of monks from Fécamp, and here they had built a monastery.

Military strength

Was the Norman army bigger and better organized than that of the English, and could this account for their victory?

The knights were the elite of the Norman army. Knights were a crucial element in the European art of war and were by no means unique to Normandy, though it was the Norman

Norman knights and English housecarls wore chain-mail shirts to protect their bodies. Chain-mail was made out of hundreds of small metal rings joined together. It was heavy to wear but afforded fairly good protection.

This delightful drawing dates from the early twelfth century. Although it depicts a soldier in Jerusalem, the conical-shaped helmet, chain-mail tunic, long lance and sword are also typical of the Norman knight at Hastings. Only the round shield is different; the Normans in 1066 favoured large kite-shaped shields.

An eleventh-century sword, almost one metre long. Usually these weapons of the nobility were long, slim and used for slashing. They weighed up to 3lbs and were worn in a wooden, leather-covered scabbard, hung at the waist

knights who enjoyed the most formidable reputation. These mounted soldiers were well-trained, well-equipped and well-paid. They wore chain-mail tunics, called hauberks, which divided at the knee to make riding easier. A metal helmet with a nasal protected their faces, while long, kite-shaped shields covered their bodies. Their chief weapons were lances or javelins for throwing, and broadswords for hacking.

The archers were a major force in the Norman army, but the English had very few. (It has been suggested that the English archers were still on their way down from Northumbria, after the Battle of Stamford Bridge, and never reached Hastings in time for the battle.) The mailed Norman archer seen here is the only mailed archer depicted in the Bayeux Tapestry. It has been suggested that he represented a crossbowman.

The two other divisions of the Norman army were the foot soldiers and the archers. The foot soldiers wore chain-mail or leather jerkins and a metal cap, and were armed with spears (thrown overarm), swords, daggers and short axes. The archers, of whom there were 1000 in William's army, were generally unmailed and used short bows. Their arrows were carried in quivers slung across their chests. These arrows made a strong impact within a range of 135 metres, but were not so effective at longer distances. It has been suggested that there may even have been some crossbowmen, represented by the one mailed archer depicted in the Bayeux Tapestry, although there is no written record of crossbows before 1098.

The Normans fought in divisions, which were sub-divided into small groups, each overseen by a baron or some other experienced military leader. William, of course, exercised ultimate control over the Norman army.

The English army was divided into two distinct groups, the housecarls and the fyrd. The housecarls were the elite of the army, the royal troops. Numbering around 3000, they were professional, well-paid, well-equipped and usually stationed near the King. They wore chain-mail similar to that of the Normans. Although they had horses, they used them only as a means of transport, rather than in battle. They were considered to be the best infantrymen in Europe and were most feared for their notorious weapon, the double-handed battle-axe – a terrible instrument which could fell a horse and rider in one blow!

The fyrd comprised the greater part of the English army and was sub-divided into the Select Fyrd and the Great Fyrd. The Select Fyrd was made up of professional soldiers who were expected to help the housecarls during an emergency. They received payment, food and equipment. The Great Fyrd consisted of ordinary men who were not trained or experienced or well-equipped. Inhabitants of each hide of land (roughly 120 acres) were expected to provide and equip one man, who was required to serve in the Fyrd for two months each year, if needed. Few of these men were mailed, and they were armed with anything that came to hand – axes, swords, daggers, stones, scythes. Local groups, or shire levies as they were known, were organized by the thegn or sheriff of the areas, but were under the ultimate command of the local earl. The potential strength of the fyrd has been estimated as being around 48,000, but it is unlikely that more than 12,000 could be organized at one time. In a time of emergency, such as in 1066, all able-bodied men were expected to turn out to fight for their King.

The two-handed Danish battle-axe was the main weapon of the English housecarls, and was reputed to be able to kill a man and his horse with one blow. Spears, thrown overarm, were the weapons of the infantry. They were made out of ash or applewood and were 2-3 metres long. Knights carried javelins and lances, which were generally thrown underarm.

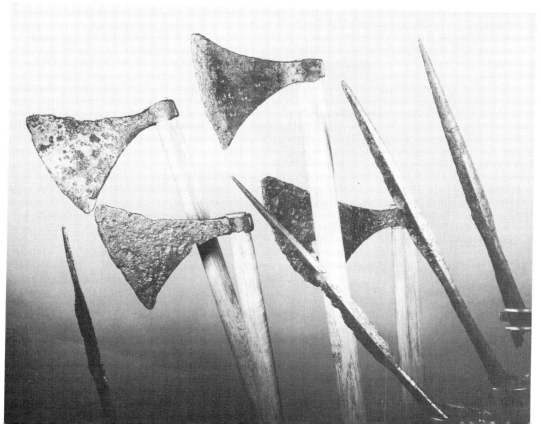

Harold's bad luck   By the beginning of September the fyrd's two months' obligatory service had long overrun, provisions were getting low and tempers were shortening. The Anglo-Saxon Chronicle records: "The provisions of the people were gone and nobody could keep them there any longer. The men were allowed to go home, and the king rode inland, and the ships were brought up to London, and many perished before they reached there."

Within two weeks of the fleet and fyrd being disbanded, Harold learnt the shocking news that Harald Hardrada had invaded Northumbria, won a victory at Gate Fulford and proclaimed himself King. Harold's instant re-assembling of the fyrd, his dramatic march north and ultimate victory at Stamford Bridge show him to have been a leader of high quality. Again, it was extreme bad luck for him that the winds in the Channel changed direction only two days after the Battle of Stamford Bridge, allowing the Normans to sail to England unopposed.

On the way down to Sussex, Harold stayed for six days in London, to rest and boost the numbers of his army. He has often been criticized for not staying longer in the capital, for had he done so, more shire levies would have been able to join the main army, and all the men would have benefited from adequate rest. Instead, Harold sacrificed numbers for speed. He arrived on Caldbec Hill with an army that was only a third of the strength Harold expected, and with men weary from gruelling marches. This was to have serious consequences.

Gyrth's plan   In London, Harold's brother Gyrth suggested an alternative plan of campaign. Realizing that Harold was exhausted, Gyrth offered to lead the army into Sussex in his stead. He pointed out that he was not bound by any oath, and that, if he should be killed, the crown would not be lost, and Harold would still be able to raise another army. This was an intelligent and practical plan, which Harold rejected angrily as dishonourable.

Tactics during the battle   During the battle William's tactics were well-thought-out. Two factors in particular have been praised: his use of the mounted knights, and the feigned retreats. The knights were excellent and accomplished horsemen, who were able to use their mounts to great advantage. Their speed and mobility were in marked contrast to the solid immobility of the English shieldwall.

Controversy surrounds the retreats, described by many of

the chroniclers. According to the French writers, only the first retreat was a genuine running away; the second, and possibly a third, were part of a deliberate plan to lure the English down from the ridge in order to massacre them. Were the French writers covering up examples of less honourable action, or were they faithfully describing a calculated manoeuvre? Military writers tend to dismiss the feigned retreats as impossible, asserting that such a sophisticated tactic could not have been used at this period, and that it would have been only too likely to turn into a real rout. But this seems to underestimate the professionalism of the Norman army, for which feigned retreats were already a recognized and successful tactic. They had been used at St Aubin le Cauf in 1053, and at Messina in 1060, with similar results to those achieved at Hastings.

Little evidence remains to tell us how Harold directed operations. He may well have authorised at least one counter-attack, maybe more. After the first, genuine Norman retreat, the fleeing knights were pursued by a large section of the fyrd, and the chaos which resulted among the Norman and Breton knights suggests that this was a deliberate counter-attack ordered by the King. If so, why did Harold not take advantage of the situation and order a mass attack? Had he done so, the battle might well have ended much sooner, with a very different result. Another frequent criticism of Harold is that he failed to order a tactical withdrawal when it became clear that victory was no longer possible: by doing so he might have saved many lives, including his own. Harold knew the country far better than William, so an escape was feasible. Instead, it seems that Harold chose death as the only honourable course.

Summary The success of the Norman army at Hastings was due to three factors: William's leadership, the composition of his army and the tactics he employed. He was in complete control of his men and throughout the campaign he acted intelligently. The mounted knights and archers were able to play a more varied and active part in the battle than Harold's solid line of men. William's tactics, including the feigned retreats, were effective. Harold was the victim of bad luck, not helped by his own impulsiveness. By sacrificing numbers for speed, he arrived on the battlefield with a depleted army of exhausted men. Luck was definitely with William, but luck alone was not enough to account for his victory. In the end, Harold was simply out-generaled.

England was conquered in one battle, for no other army

was organized to challenge William. The reason seems to have been that there was no Englishman left who would be capable of assembling and leading a large army – the majority of the aristocracy having been killed in the three battles of 1066. The only possible candidates, the earls Morcar and Edwin, were still in their teens. Weary with fighting, and in the belief that survival depended on keeping a low profile, they soon retreated to Northumbria. Edgar, the royal prince, was only a child and was only briefly considered by the Witan as Harold's successor. Finally, William seemed the only viable ruler, for, as the biographer of Wulfstan of Worcester recorded, "It was as though with Harold had fallen also the whole strength of the country."

What were the consequences of the Conquest?

Normanization
The most obvious effect of the Conquest was that England acquired a foreign King, who proved to be the first of a new dynasty. French-speaking descendants of William were on the throne until 1399, when Henry IV became the first King since Harold II to have English as his mother-tongue.

Since the majority of the English aristocracy had lost their lives during the three battles of 1066, William was able to redistribute their titles and lands to his own supporters, as a reward for their help. Within a few years, England was therefore governed by a small alien minority who owned almost all of the country's land and wealth. The new rulers were in a potentially dangerous situation and Norman authority was enforced through a harsh military rule, with William and his barons working in close co-operation. The dominance of this small group, approximately 2 per cent of the population, was achieved at the expense of the old Anglo-Danish aristocracy, which had been virtually annihilated.

Between 1066 and 1090 over 200,000 French and Norman settlers arrived in England, and many of them inter-married with the native population. They introduced a completely new culture and a new language, and they totally reformed both society and Church. Again, this was achieved at the expense of Saxon traditions and, by the end of William's reign in 1087, all things English were considered old-fashioned and inferior. William of Malmesbury, writing in 1125, summed up the feelings of the native population: "England is become the residence of foreigners and the property of aliens. At the present time there is no English earl, nor bishop nor abbot. Strangers all they [the Normans] prey upon the riches and vitals of England."

Suppression and resistance
Although William had won a decisive victory at Hastings and had established himself firmly on the throne, he could not claim to be in complete control of the country until 1081. The first five years of his reign were marked by almost continual rebellion in one area or another. In 1067 the men of the south-west rose in revolt. In 1069 there was a northern uprising and an unwelcome visit from Swein of Denmark. In 1070 Swein led a larger invasion force to England, the North revolted

hIC   DOMVS:IN CENDITVR: hIC:MIL

To subdue rebellious areas, William authorised a policy of deliberate terrorism, putting land and people to fire and the sword. This scene from the Bayeux Tapestry represents what took place in Sussex shortly after the arrival of the Norman army, but similar actions occurred in Yorkshire during 1069-70.

again, and Hereward the Wake waged guerrilla war against the Normans from the Fens of East Anglia. In each case William's reaction was swift and merciless: the rebellions were quickly put down and the offending areas put to fire and the sword. This policy had devastating effects, particularly in the north, where 1000 square miles were turned into a wilderness. Orderic Vitalis grimly noted: "In the fullness of his wrath he [William] ordered the corn and cattle, with the implements of husbandry and provisions of every sort, to be collected in great heaps and set on fire, until the whole was consumed, and thus destroyed at once all that could serve for the support of life in the whole country lying north of the Humber." During William's reign, over 300,000 English men, women and children died as a result of battle, starvation or murder – that was one in five of the population. The submission of the native population was gained by introducing harsh military rule based on feudalism.

Feudalism Feudalism being the system of government and social organization used in Normandy, it was both logical and desirable for William to introduce this system, which he understood, into his new realm. Although some historians now believe that a form of feudalism may have existed already in England in the mid-eleventh century, this would have been by no means as rigid or as militaristic as the regime later introduced by the Normans.

Feudalism was a system of land grants and obligations which bound one man to another. The man granting the land was known as the "lord", and the man receiving the land the "vassal".

After the Conquest, William made it clear that he considered himself to be Edward the Confessor's rightful successor, and as such he took all land as his royal due. Although he kept more than 1000 manors (estates) for himself, William gave large grants of land (honours) to his most prestigious followers, as rewards for their services. The receivers of honours did not own the land but held it from the King; they were known as tenants-in-chief, and were usually earls, barons and bishops. The tenants-in-chief then sub-divided the honours into smaller portions of land (fiefs) and granted these in turn to their supporters, who became known as tenants. Tenants were usually knights.

The lands were not given lightly. In each case, the tenant was required to swear an oath of allegiance (fealty) to his lord and to fulfil certain military services. Tenants were expected to train and maintain a certain number of knights for use by the King. The number varied from estate to estate but was generally based on multiples of five – a small manor providing five knights, for example, while a greater manor would be responsible for forty or fifty knights. Even bishops were expected to keep armed men in exchange for their lands. William estimated that he therefore had at least 5000 knights available to him if necessary. The knights became a new and elitist military class upon whom feudalism depended.

The peasants (villeins) were also drawn into the feudal system. In exchange for the right to farm strips of land in a manor, they were expected also to work the lord's land on a certain number of days each week, and to pay him taxes and dues.

The result was a carefully structured society where every man had a master. Pyramidal in shape, a feudal society ensured that all were ultimately bound through oaths of loyalty and grants of land to the lord of lords – the King, who, if strong enough, was able to wield considerable power. William was such a King, and through him feudalism provided an efficient means by which a minority could govern a majority.

Castles However, an uneasy peace was maintained only by relying heavily on the military aspects of feudalism, and therefore it has often been regarded as an oppressive regime. Knights were used to "police" areas in which they were based, and were living symbols of the King's authority. Other symbols of that authority were the new Norman castles. Before 1066 there were only four castles in England, all of which had been built by Normans resident in the country. By the end of William's reign there were over 80, and by 1120 over 500 castles had been built at strategically important points throughout England. The earlier castles, such as Hastings and Dover, were wooden buildings erected on a mound of earth (motte) surrounded by a ditched and embanked outer courtyard (bailey). By the 1080s, castles were being built from stone and afforded excellent protection to the resident lord and his retainers.

Development of government

The Normans were not great innovators, but they were excellent organizers and administrators. Generally, they took over existing institutions and adapted or improved them. This was very much the case in England. William was anxious to be seen as Edward's true successor and was eager to inherit the English throne as it stood, complete with all its rights and privileges. Combining the established monarchy with feudal concepts enhanced the position of the King and gave the monarch more power than he had ever previously enjoyed. Many of the old institutions of government were retained, but the new posts of Chancellor and Treasurer were introduced. The original financial system remained intact, as did the coinage; and although many new laws were brought in, the majority of the old Saxon ones stayed unchanged. At a local level, government continued uninterrupted, with shires, hundreds and wapentakes still the bases of administration.

Berkhamsted Castle was one of the first castles to be built after the Conquest, and was given to William's half-brother, Robert Mortain. It is of a motte and bailey design, and is remarkable for having the only known example of a double moat.

The West Front of Ely Cathedral. Perched on high, in the middle of the Isle of Ely, this beautiful cathedral was built in the early twelfth century, and still retains some magnificent examples of Norman architecture. The twelfth-century work here is identifiable by the round arches of the windows and pillars. (The top of the tower and the porch are later additions.) Originally there was also a north wing to correspond with the existing south wing, but the latter fell some time during the fifteenth century.

Reorganization of the Church

During 1066, many churchmen had died or fled, leaving vacant sees, offices and land. These offices were slowly filled, under the direction of William and his new Archbishop of Canterbury, Lanfranc. Because the new men were carefully selected, greater unity was achieved in the Church and new enthusiasm was created. Dioceses were reorganized and brought in line with the Continental system, and under Lanfranc's primacy, Canterbury became the focal point of the Church, the Archbishop of York having to swear allegiance to him.

The "flowering" of the Church was perhaps most apparent in architecture, as the Romanesque, or Norman, style was introduced. It had only been seen in England before in Westminster Abbey and Waltham Abbey. During the Norman period (1066-1154), large numbers of cathedrals were built, including St Albans, Canterbury, Durham and Ely, as were many monasteries and abbeys, among them Rievaulx and Tewkesbury. Virtually all churches from before 1066 were remodelled, and hundreds of new parish churches were built. William of Malmesbury described how the Normans ". . . revived the rule of religion which had grown lifeless" and he admiringly noted that "you might see churches rise in every village . . . monasteries built in a style never seen before; you might watch the country flourish with renewed religious observance."

England into Europe   The final and far-reaching effect of the Conquest was to break England's Scandinavian ties and make the country part of Latin Europe. This had the most profound cultural, economic and political consequences.

Summary   To finish, here are three views to consider: one contemporary, one modern and one supposedly from William himself.

The Anglo-Saxon Chronicle: "King William of whom we speak, was a man of great wisdom and power, and surpassed in honour and in strength all those who had gone before him. Though stern beyond measure to those who opposed his will, he was kind to those good men who loved God. . . . During his reign was built the great cathedral at Canterbury and many another throughout England. . . . Moreover he kept a great state. . . . He was so stern and relentless a man that no one dared do aught against his will . . . we must not forget the good

A closer view of the south wing of Ely Cathedral.

A life-size model of William I, which was on display at the Public Record Office's exhibition on Domesday in 1986. The figure has been carefully based on contemporary accounts of William's appearance.

A silver penny from the reign of William I, possibly minted in Dover. It is the only known contemporary likeness of the new King.

order he kept in the land, so that a man of any substance could travel unmolested throughout the country with his bosom full of gold."

Maurice Ashley, from "The Life and Times of William I": William's rule "introduced a somewhat wider culture but it contributed little to the happiness of the bulk of King William's subjects; the Conquest was achieved at a terrible cost out of all proportion to the benefits it concurred."

William I, on his deathbed: "I persecuted the native inhabitants of England beyond all reason; whether nobles or commons I cruelly oppressed them; many I unjustly disinherited; innumerable multitudes, especially in the county of York, perished through me by famine and sword. I am stained with the rivers of blood I have shed." (From Orderic Vitalis, *Historia Ecclesiastica*)

Further reading

PRIMARY SOURCES

The Bayeux Tapestry
The Bayeux Tapestry is believed to have been worked in England, probably in Kent, between 1067 and 1082, at the behest of Odo, Bishop of Bayeux. It is a long strip of embroidery, 68.38m long and between 45.7 and 53.6cm wide. Rather like a modern strip cartoon, it depicts events which occurred from 1064 to the Battle of Hastings. The only missing part is the end, which may well have shown the coronation of William. Embroideries like this were a common means of recording a notable event. The finished tapestry probably hung in Bayeux Cathedral and today it can still be seen in Bayeux, now housed in a special museum. A reproduction of the tapestry is on display in the Victoria and Albert Museum, London. The Reading Art Gallery and Museum also has a facsimile which is sometimes on display (for further details ring 0734 575911 ext 2242). Numerous books contain photographs of the entire embroidery; the best is by David Wilson, published by Thames and Hudson.

William of Poitiers: "Gesta Guillelmi Ducis Normannorum et Regis Anglorum" ("The Story of William Duke of Normandy and King of England")
Written in 1073 by the Duke's chaplain, this account gives an interesting and reliable description of the battle and events leading up to it. Though not actually present at the battle, William of Poitiers was in a position to receive first-hand information. A translation of this work can be found in Lewis Thorpe's book *The Bayeux Tapestry and the Norman Invasion*, published by the Folio Society, 1973.

Guy of Amiens: "Carmen de Hastingae Proelio" ("Story of the Battle of Hastings")
Possibly written around 1068, this is not generally taken as reliable history, but it remains a readable and enjoyable account of what might have happened. A translation by H. Muntz and C. Morton is published by Oxford University Press, 1972.

The Anglo-Saxon Chronicle
The Anglo-Saxon Chronicle exists in six manuscripts, written by different people but each containing much the same information. The Chronicle tells the history of Britain year by year, from Julius Caesar's invasion in 55 BC to 1154 AD. It is the only contemporary English source and has useful material on Stamford Bridge as well as Hastings. Several translations are available, including one by G.N. Garmondsay, London, 1953. Four of the original manuscripts are in the British Museum, and the two others are in Oxford and Cambridge.

William of Jumièges: "Gesta Normannorum Ducum" ("A History of the Dukes of Normandy")

This history was written around 1070, while William was a monk at one of the principal Norman abbeys, possibly at Rouen. It consists of 8 books and covers the history of the Norman dukes up to 1135 (the later parts being added by other writers). The 7th book covers the period of the Battle of Hastings and gives a straightforward and reliable account of the battle.

William of Malmesbury: "Gesta Regum Anglorum" ("History of the Kings of England")

William of Malmesbury was born in the late eleventh century and, as his name implies, probably in the West Country. Of mixed parentage, he claimed impartiality in his account of the battle and subsequent events, although it tends to be pro-English. The *Gesta* was written in 1125.

Robert Wace: "Le Roman de Rou" ("The Romance of Rollo")

Wace was born in Jersey, but studied in Paris and later became a cleric in Caen in Normandy. He was commissioned by Henry II to write a poem about the battle of Hastings. The result was the *Roman*, written some time between 1160 and 1174. It was written in French-Norman verse and is more literature than historical fact. It is very anti-Harold but makes enjoyable reading.

Chronicle of Battle Abbey

This was written in the late twelfth century by an anonymous monk from the Abbey. It covers the years 1066-1176.

Orderic Vitalis: "Historia Ecclesiastica" ("History of the Church")

Orderic Vitalis was born in Shrewsbury in 1075. Like William of Malmesbury, he was of mixed parentage. He spent most of his life as a monk in a monastery near Lisieux in Normandy and wrote the *Ecclesiastica* between 1123 and 1141. It contains good descriptions of both Stamford Bridge and Hastings. It is very pro-English and sympathetic towards Harold, and is unusual in that it has Harold dying in the early stages of the battle. Much is cribbed from William of Poitiers and William of Jumièges, though.

"Brevis Relatio de Origine Willelmi"

This brief but accurate account of the battle was written during the twelfth century. Nothing is known about the author.

"Vita Aedwardi Regis" ("Life of King Edward")

A description of the life of Edward the Confessor, written anonymously in the twelfth century. It includes a good account of the events at Edward's deathbed. The *Vita* has has been translated by F. Barlow (Nelson, 1962).

Florence of Worcester: "Chronicon ex Chronicis"
Written in the twelfth century by an admirer of Harold, this tells the story of the English, from the arrival of Horsa and Hengist in the fifth century up to 1117. It gives an English view of the events surrounding Hastings.

Translations of all or parts of the documents mentioned are available in *English Historical Documents* Vol III (Oxford, 1957), *The Norman Conquest, Documents of Medieval History* 5 (Edward Arnold, 1984) and *Hastings Castle* Vol. II by Dawson (London, 1909). All are obtainable from larger libraries or through a specific order.

SECONDARY SOURCES

The Field of Hastings, Col. C.M. Lemmon, Budd and Gillat, 1957
The Norman Conquest, M.E. Reeves, Longman, 1973
The Life and Times of William I, Maurice Ashley, Weidenfeld and Nicolson, 1973
The Normans, "Peoples of the Past" series, MacDonald, 1977
Norman Britain, Henry Loyn and Alan Sorrel, Lutterworth Press, 1977
Growing Up during the Norman Conquest, Frances Wilkins, Batsford

Glossary

Aethling	Anglo-Saxon for Prince.
bailey	outer courtyard area of a castle.
baron	a tenant-in-chief of the King, holding land in return for military services.
danegeld	a tax on land, first levied to buy off the Danes, later an annual peacetime tax.
Danelaw	the part of England settled and administered by the Danes, including East Anglia, Yorkshire, etc.
feudalism	medieval system of government and social organization, based on a network of mutual rights and obligations linking lords and vassals.
fief	manor granted to vassal by lord.
fyrd	Anglo-Saxon militia.
gonfanon	banner.
hauberk	chain-mail tunic.
hide	land division, approximately 120 acres.
homage	oath of fidelity, made by vassal to lord.
housecarl	elite, professional English warrior in the King's service.
hundred	unit of local government, originally 100 hides.
lord	feudal superior of a vassal.
mercenary	professional soldier who hires out his services for payment.
motte	earth mound upon which a castle was erected.
nasal	nose-piece of a helmet.
palisade	sturdy fence of pointed stakes.
perjurer	oath-breaker.
primogeniture	system by which the eldest son of a family inherits property etc.
romanesque	style of architecture, characterized by round arches and columns.
sheriff	chief official charged with administering a shire or county.
shieldwall	a solid line of shields touching or overlapping.
shire levy	local branch of the fyrd.
standard	banner.
thegn	lord in pre-Norman England.
tribute	payment of money, usually to a stronger or superior party.
usurper	person who has stolen a position rightfully belonging to someone else.
vassal	in feudalism, person who owes allegiance and service to a lord.
villeins	peasant class, bound to a lord through land-holding and tenure duties.
wapentake	Danelaw equivalent to a hundred.
witan	advisory council to King in Anglo-Saxon England.

Index